seeking the other side

seeking the other side

poems by jane olmsted

 Fleur-de-Lis Press   Louisville, Kentucky   2015

Copyright © 2015 Jane Olmsted

All rights reserved. No part of this book may be reproduced in any form or by any electronic or mechanical means including information storage and retrieval systems without permission in writing from the author, except by a revier who may quote brief passages in a review. Please direct requests to Fleur-de-Lis Press, 851 S. Fourth Street, Louisville, Kentucky 40203

Cover art: *Braced*, by Yvonne Petkus
Book design by Jonathan Weinert

Printed in the United States of America
First Edition

Library of Congress Cataloging-in-Publication Data
Olmsted, Jane.
Seeking the Other Side.
I. Title
Library of Congress Control Number: 2015937290

ISBN 978-0-9773861-8-5

Fleur-de-Lis Press of *The Louisville Review*
Spalding University
851 S. Fourth Street
Louisville, KY 40203
502.873.4398
louisvillereview@spalding.edu
www.louisvillereview.org

Contents

Acknowledgments   vi
Introduction   vii
Prologue   x

ways of touching

    A Body of Poetry   3
    Pathetic Fallacy   4
    Our Shadows Race Lengthwise   5
    Naming the Flowers   7
    Artist at Five   12
    Cicada   14
    Dream of Extraordinary Ease   17
    Roadside Encounter   18
    Far, Far Away, in Vilnius   22
    Confession   23
    Someone Else's Offspring   25
    The Shape and Size of Things   27
    After   28
    Kodiak Ghazal   30
    Two White Pigeons   31
    Whisper   33

tree forms

Bulky Thing   37

Camping on Greys River, Bridger Tetons   38

Aspen Hieroglyphs   40

Pando   41

On Disappointment   42

When I Fall   43

Who Listens to an Old Woman?   45

Write My Back   47

Sitting at My Uncle's Window   48

Bad Habits   51

The Story They Tell Is Our Story   53

These Things Left Behind   55

Oak Tree at the Window   57

Intrusion   58

The Hole   59

Heart of the Matter   62

the casey poems

Blessed by the Dalai Lama   67

Cyan   68

Imperative   70

Hydrostatic Shock   72

The Tree You Come Home To   74

Things That Are Hot and Cold   76

Minor Chord   77

Twenty-One Tomorrow   79

Memento Mori   80

Rogue Tongue   82

Ghazal, by a Thread   83

The Weight of a Human Heart   84

Architecture of Loss   86

Second Year   88

Requiem for the Bristlecone Pine at Lake Haiyaha   90

About the Author   99

About the Cover Artist   100

Acknowledgments

I am grateful to the editors of the following publications, where these poems first appeared:

"Someone Else's Offspring," "Far, Far Away, in Vilnius," "Confession," and "Two White Pigeons," *The Journal of Kentucky Studies*, September 2012.

"The Tree You Come Home To," *The Scream Online*, Fall 2011.

"Kodiak Ghazal," *5x5*, June 2011.

Tree Forms, chapbook, Finishing Line Press, June 2011.

"Ghazal, by a Thread," *Innisfree Poetry Journal*, 12, March 2011.

"Imperative," finalist, Vivienne Haigh-Wood Poetry Prize, *Melusine*, April 2010.

"Pathetic Fallacy," *Adirondack Review*, June 2007.

"Roadside Encounter," *Barnwood Magazine*, Fall 2006.

"Dream of Extraordinary Ease," *Slow Trains*, December 2005.

"Cicada," *Writing Who We Are: Poems by Kentucky Feminists*, WKU, 1999.

"Naming the Flowers," *Nimrod International Journal of Prose and Poetry*, volume 35, no. 1, Fall/Winter 1991.

"Our Shadows Race Lengthwise," *Poetry Northwest*, Fall 1978.

I also wish to thank my poet friends who offered suggestions on this collection at various times—Elizabeth Oakes, Mary Ellen Miller, Barbara Wade, and Dorothy Schnare. Heartfelt thanks to Yvonne Petkus for her art and especially to Sena Jeter Naslund and Maureen Morehead for many years of friendship, support, and mutual respect.

Introduction

So many things to say about this extraordinary collection of poems, but difficult to find the right words. Perhaps because I've known Jane Olmsted for years, know when she wrote her early poems, had her first child, earned her degrees, found her voice for speaking for those without a voice . . . that it's simply painful to introduce the poems that emerged from my friend's grave pain.

And yet, it's often human suffering that compels the poet to break silence, to seek answers to the most fundamental questions, to brave trauma head-on, and to invite the reader to share the quest that gives these poems such weight and high purpose.

I have been thinking for some time about what Gregory Orr calls "the poetry of survival," how the very act of arranging words on a page is a way of addressing the terrible decentering effects of the tragic events in our lives. Writing a lyric poem compels the poet to create intricate patterns. "This patterning necessitates, among other things," writes Orr in *Poetry as Survival*, "careful attention to accurate and economical word choice, to the expressive possibilities of rhythm, to the dramatic unfolding of story, and to the descriptive vividness and symbolic power of details."[1] For one in pain, the distraction of putting together what has been torn apart is a welcome release.

It is also selfless work. When a poet turns to the lyric, breaking her silence in the aftermath of trauma, she is stating her faith in art. She knows transforming her grief into song may bring light and hope to a reader who is suffering likewise. Recognizing herself in the poem, the reader feels connected, less isolated: "When the poem succeeds in incorporating disorder without disintegrating into chaos or silence, I, the reader, am given both courage and hope." Acknowledging the importance of the reader, the poet knows intuitively, is an act of empathy, love.

I could write in detail about the quality of each poem's language and structure, of how Jane has mastered line and symbol, sound and form, how she successfully creates metaphors to express the ineffable, and has invited the reader to share in her quest to find "the other side." The last poem, "Requiem of the Bristlecone Pine at Lake Haiyaha," is an exquisite elegy, keeping close the poet's pain, but seeking consolation as she lays down word after word:

> Already your torments have lost their sting
> and your good works follow you.
>
> We speak of being better people
> and set our timid feet upon the ground.
>
> I begin to see that when peace enters
> its succor will not pervade
>
> that nothing will stay the loss of you except you
> in your new form, moving and yet still.

What I find equally compelling about *Seeking the Other Side* is that Jane has set her son's murder within the context of his twenty years of life, presenting him in poems as she knows him, her youngest, alternately sweet and troubled, the father of a young child, a member of a real family, each grieving his loss in his or her own way.

With context provided, it became clear to me that a central theme in this collection is that the past is shaped by the present, particularly in the event of great loss. Just as T.S. Eliot posits in "Tradition and the

Individual Talent," a new poem added to the canon changes those poems that came before, Jane writes that an act of violence against one's child can affect even one's memories; even memories of a long, solid marriage may pale, endangering the bond of the sacrament.

The poems comprising the final section of the book and detailing the specifics of the murder surprised me with their style, so different from the older poems. It's as if this new frontier required a new language and form to tell the story. Most obvious are the prose poems that report medical and forensic information released in the days and months after the crime. Other new poems, written in more conventional free verse, are direct and clear, less figurative than earlier poems, as if the poet wants to make certain she is understood. The poems leave the genre of elegy to enter the political arena. Jane questions, for example, the "right to bear arms" as those arms seem to often find their way into the hands of "madmen" who horde weapons, along with irrepressible anger toward everything.

Remarkably, having presented nature throughout the book as a spiritual haven, Jane chose for these final poems language that speaks of her son in words he would appreciate, the language of Christianity. Reported in the autopsy, a tattoo on one arm shows "Jesus' head, bent, hands carrying a wooden cross." On the other, "his daughter's face accented by red roses, her little hand folded under her chin." And it becomes a language that Jane Olmsted assumes for her private journey toward light, as these are ultimately sacred poems, and those of us who enter them walk with the poet on sacred ground.

—Maureen Morehead
Author of *Late August Blues: The Daylily Poems*

1. Orr, Gregory. 2002. *Poetry as Survival*. Athens: University of Georgia Press.

Prologue

In 2009, I began to learn the meaning of grief, loss, regret. I am not finished exploring that shifting terrain, but I do know that when we face a very great loss, it makes a great difference how we come to understand the experience and describe it—to others, but most importantly, perhaps, to ourselves.

I took up poetry again, after years of setting it aside for other matters. A deluge of images and jumbled phrases filled my head. I had to put pen to paper, image to word . . . and eventually, to share the poems with others. But I was stricken by the suspicion that I was using the intensity of feeling and image that arose from the terrible rending of our lives for personal (or worse, professional) benefit. With every poem I polished and sent off for publication, I worried that I was capitalizing on the very worst thing that ever happened to us.

I take heart in Audre Lorde's description of what happens when we examine the fears we carry around, when we refuse to silence ourselves despite the doubts we harbor about our ability to speak with meaning, and to trust that our little bit of meaning matters—at least to someone. In fact, I'm coming to realize how much every action is premised by and builds upon a rampant, unbridled trust—that what we love most won't be, tomorrow, gone—the whisper of rain, birdsong before sunrise, our children's voices, even the possibility of a future.

While Lorde is talking to black women (her primary audience), her work offers wisdom to all of us who find our way to her. In her essay "Poetry Is Not a Luxury," she speaks of the "dark place within where hidden and growing our true spirit rises," despite the denial and silencing of oppressive ideologies. While his audience is different, David Orr speaks of the same sort of dark place from which our spirits shine, when he talks about "the sense of awe toward the creation [that] had a great deal to do with the origin of language and why early humans wanted to talk, sing, and write poetry in the first place."[1] If we accept the possibility that our poetic roots go back to our first rubbing of a blackened stick on a cave wall, then it must certainly be important to nurture that impulse. Lorde asks that we recognize (black women and all of us) and then honor those feelings that have been routinely slapped aside as irrelevant; when we make this conscious decision, we have taken the first step to fashioning a way to connect to ourselves (the heart, the body) and to each other.

So elemental is our connection with the stuff of nature that a mere touch electrifies, a smell becomes a stab of memory transporting us to a time long buried. After weeks of drought, the early morning light kisses a rain-spattered plant and our eyes fill with tears. Unprepared for the sudden stab in the heart, we are transported from the mundane to the sacred that always resides somewhere inside the predictable. Put another way, David Abrams, in *The Spell of the Sensuous*, says, "For the largest part of our species' existence, humans have negotiated relationships with every aspect of the sensuous surroundings, exchanging possibilities with every flapping form, with each textured surface and shivering entity that we happened to focus on. All could speak, articulating in gesture and whistle and sigh a shifting web of meanings that we felt on our skin or inhaled through our nostrils or focused on with our listening ears, and to which we replied."[2]

I call this collection *Seeking the Other Side* as a way to reinvigorate what acquisitiveness and obsessive work habits deaden—the capacity to connect in some way with the Other, even when that turns out to be a part of ourselves. I hope in these poems to reach through or across the boundaries that keep us ignorant of truths beyond the readily apparent.

I think of the "other side" not just as what's across the line between life and death, between myself and my son, but as what's across any other real or illusory line that stifles access to the fullness of life.

The three sections are only partially chronological. Some of my oldest poems are in Part I—Ways of Touching—as is my most recent poem, "Whisper." I realized in compiling the collection, that touching is a powerful way of reaching out, as well as of receiving. Touch may be physical, of the hand or of the eyes or ears—any of the senses—but it can also express a spiritual longing, loneliness, as well as humor and joy, embodied and known to us as a rapid heartbeat or a bubbling sensation or a dark weight. The act of reaching out is an act of bridge-building, and I can almost visualize the arches as they rise and fall between us.

Part II—Tree Forms—contains the poems of my 2011 chapbook by the same name, with some exceptions and minor revisions. I began the series about a month before Casey died, when I was on sabbatical camping in the Rockies and searching for some answers to those sorts of questions that keep us wondering and seeking. I began photographing the trees, which were beautiful or strange, peculiar and sometimes ugly, at least at first glance. Many of them seemed to be telling a story—or was it my own story they were giving back? When I returned home my fascination with "tree forms" continued, and this section offers poems that came to me, in some cases, when sadness was the only place I could recognize.

The Requiem poem that ends the collection was inspired by the most fantastic of the trees, the bristlecone pine, situated on the shore of Lake Haiyaha, fed by Chaos Creek. Every photograph I took of the old bristlecone looks as if it belongs to a different tree, such are the turns and twists of its limbs. I imagined it as a family tree. Remarkably, the *Pinus aristas* is the longest lived of organisms, reaching 4,000 years and more. What might such a tree have to say about the sudden and violent end of someone so young? The seven-part poem is inspired by Johannes Brahms' *Requiem*, which was my mother's favorite piece of music, and what I listened to repeatedly over the first two years. The other poems in the final section—The Casey Poems—tell a story of healing, another "side" I desperately needed to find from the place of suffering. These poems seek understanding, beauty, most eloquently expressed in the small, the simple, the truly sacred.

—*Jane Olmsted*

1. Orr, David. 2004. *Earth in Mind: On Education, Environment, and the Human Prospect.* Washington: Island Press.
2. Abrams, David. 1996. *The Spell of the Sensuous: Perception and Language in a More-Than-Human World.* New York: Vintage Books.

For Casey and Leah,
all ways, always.

ways of touching

A Body of Poetry

Rust in the crevices of this pen
spurs on the bony page:
this voice ragged
with pneumatic air—

Two decades of grafting voice
onto obligation—*oh,*
but there was joy, wasn't there?—
sending out the archivist's
erotic whispers.

Or did it grow small and dense
and lodge in the recesses of the throat?

Beneath the aching rib a shadow beckons.

Pathetic Fallacy

Last night I saw it hanging
from the branches
of my walnut tree,
throttled by the wind
and beat up as an old baseball glove.

This morning I thought I saw it
in the street,
somehow missed by neighbors' cars,
a pathetic thing scurrying away
from approaching tires.

Runaway, it leaves
a fluorescent cavity
large enough to hold a fist—

Tonight I look for it in the trees,
in neighbors' curbside mailboxes.
I return home empty-chested,
breathe into the pillowcase
spiraled as an ear.

Outside hail big as baseballs
smacks the windows
gets to the heart of things
sends most animals running home.

Our Shadows Race Lengthwise

We fall into bed together—
I am not sure you can feel it,
then you say,
"I have been waiting."

The sheets are so far away below my hands—
I reach for them.
I am certain that if I touch them
this nausea will fade . . .

The cat crawls over our chests.
She thinks it's a night for hunting,
that we are the hills behind the cemetery—
nothing I can say will stop her.

We lie still like the pages of reworked poetry
that fall in about the bed.
In my mind I pick them up,
organize them, extracting necessary lines—

"The moss crept up like fingers over the ledge,
ready to grow and cover us—
we were too eager."

Our hips become tumbled boulders
whose shadows race lengthwise out the window.

The cat peers down the long ravine
watching our hands for unsuspecting mice and grouse.

Nausea rolls across the windowsill, falling heavily.
Sheets glimmer below my gaze to the cemetery
where an angel lifts her heavy wings toward the hills
leaving veil and moonwhite slippers to the night.

Naming the Flowers

In any field, in the shade of any sagging porch—
here in Berea they grow thick, if you know where to look.
Roll the Rs in your mouth, let the sour drops clink
against your teeth: moor of maureen
grows at the edges of marshes
green frogs croak there and slide up and down her stalks
like accordion music,
old fashioned dorothies can be heated and drunk
like Earl Grey, and no one's the wiser;
the As melt beneath your tongue, mossy and sweet:
barbara's breath, gloriander
grow elbow deep in the shade of Lincoln.
I reach my hands in and pull out blossoms
thick as dish suds, set them in amethyst vases on my desk.
Students come in bewildered but leave
with the breath of wisdom like pollen
on the hairy knobs of their knees.
Some sniff the air—"have you been burning incense?"
Two or three see them, their hands hover over them.
One says, "Oh, you've got those pretty little flowers again.
Where do you find them?"
I impart my best knowledge: "Oh, well, you know," I say.

Last week I saw the first keila lilies
growing along Brushy Fork—anything growing there
needs to be strong—I cut long stalks, pile them in a large urn.
I set them in the dining room

on the floor in the corner, hide beneath them,
their orange petals like long foreign bangs.
I squat ready to pee, and I would too if I were
at the edge of Scaffold Cane or next to the running path,
but I've only just taught my son not to pee
in the heating vent. He wouldn't understand
the double standard, so I hold it in,
and when the dog passes I lunge at him.
He runs in terror, ears flat as geography, his claws skipping
across the linoleum. Now he's on two legs
his hips sweeping the floor ahead of him.
When he peers at me from behind the bar, I stand at the sink
as if nothing has happened.
In a few minutes I will pat his head.
I don't want to leave anyone bewildered for too long.

I stand with the lilies pointing toward earth.
Eight men are hoeing the College gardens,
their eight straight sticks swing in offbeat unison,
slashing the petals at their feet.
They see only the land to be cultivated.
I call out for them to stop, but I am caught in the image:
their backs, graceful as the wheaty stalks of peggy pods
before the wind catches her seeds and blows them
to kingdom come,
glisten red and brown, lulling. My breath catches.
The nearest one has his shirt tucked into a rear pocket,

the way I like.
I creep up, kiss his neck,
lick his shoulder blades, cup the pectorals.
My hands slide down his stomach, the few stray hairs,
to his loosened belt. I hear the suck of air, nibble his ears.
He looks up, sees me in the cinders, nods his head,
the way men do, politely. I nod back,
wonder what he'd say.
Before I leave I whisper the enchantment to restore life to my sisters,
to protect them from this prodigious mowing.
I'll teach it to you now:
Stretch out both arms, fingers extended so no power escapes.
Lower your eyelids to a squint, to the sultry heavy-lashed look
of a sex starved goddess, so that your vision blurs.
Then speak the spell.
You know the words. You know.

A cold sweat wakes me.
I check my children, their arms flung out
their lips parted. My husband snores peacefully.
Yet my scalp tingles and I hear them distinctly:
the baying and snarling, the spell breakers, the hounds.
I slip off my nightgown, I have learned—
if you are to face them be as naked as you can get,
and get the help of your friends.
I tie a bandana around my left thigh and step out.
A full moon pours over my breasts and ass, over

the flowers, for it is night in Berea, when they migrate and bloom,
flock from the pinnacles through fences
as determined as morning glories.
They greet me with whispers and sighs,
they've been waiting for me to come out and play.
Laughing, I weave diana daisies,
dripping with moonglow,
dorothies' leaves and barbara's breath
delicate as china.
I am gentle as I can be with them,
tuck in a keila lily or two, some peggy pods,
rose of maureen,
and set the wreath upon my head.

I am up to my elbows in mary ann's hips and red libby's lips.
They tie themselves like dancer's bells
at my ankles and wrists.
I spin, ringing out, catch sight of the yellow frame house.
It breathes a welcome to me, says come back to bed,
but at its edges I see eyes cold as shaved glass
in a frozen cocktail.
My eyes spring to a flower I have missed,
perhaps it's just arriving, taking some years to get here.
I touch the black petals as streaked with gray
as my friends' hair.
I rub its petals, using only my thumb and first finger
to pull out the aloe vera.

I rub the oil on my face,
slick down my arms, dripping now,
baby orchids sprouting at my feet.
Oiled and slippery as a fish I fling the liquid
out of my fenced yard.
The street is a frenzy of dark orchids.
Drenched, my hair long as jubilation, I arch my shoulders
and dance backwards.
In the distance dogs yap, the way some do
when a cat they haven't noticed gets up and stretches.

Artist at Five

I sit in the corner of our sofa
pat my left hip
and no matter what he's doing
he leaps to that easy perch
pen in hand—

beneath each floating flower
or clog of mossy river grass
fuzzy roots give birth
to crayola green creatures
who press to their magenta hearts
the hearts of others,
breathing, eating, farting purple bubbles
that rise to the surface and explode,
great looping patterns;

and in his eyes he is testing to see if I understand:
smiling his gappy smile,
four teeth missing, falling out of one accord
like friends not wanting to stand
in the middle of that block alone
when the rest of the gang has gone.

For now this is who he is for me:
excess of loyalty and laughter
overflowing a bright container.
Bony knees jab my stomach

hands grip each side of my head
his face pushes into my face
noses flatten—

In his scowls I see my own
as I see in mine my mother's.
For him I undo my face
unknot it frame by frame.

Cicada

I   IN THE CARE OF THE BABYSITTER

Robert finds the emerging cicada
on the edge of a piece of bark
above the children's heads, above their swing.
They watch the wings rolled up as rice
and the black slippers pull
the oversized body out of its dull husk.
It emerges from a deep sleep
groggy and full of the other world.
One boy reaches for it,
but Robert stops his hand at the wrist,
"You can't touch it."
"Yeah, you'll kill it," says his brother,
his hands dancing an arabesque nearby.

The wings begin to unfold.
I imagine the pain: each fiber burns
as it stretches away from the protective custody
of each neighboring cell—
there is no turning back now,
no return to the scabby mold.

Cicada doesn't know how lucky it is.

II METAMORPHOSIS

Across town, I am describing how much our babysitter has grown
this first year away from home, trying to find the words
to describe how well he fits his body,
as if a year ago he merely rattled around inside his skin—
or in his own coming of age
he stood up to that harsh unfurling
and found himself taller, his back straight.

This transformation takes seven years, they say.
Right now my oldest heads down the homestretch
to his seventh birthday and I wonder
what growing pains first grade will bring.
Seven years ago I began a marriage,
offered the world two lives,
and now another,
said, "Here, I trust you to care for these
they are mine I would not have them destroyed."

Already I feel an itching at my shoulder blades
where I can't quite reach the scaly skin
though I can just make out the V through the steam
where my rubbing in the bathroom mirror
has left a filmy reflection.
Any day now I shall lay myself down
pull my body into its tightening shell,

trusting the stillness to remain free
from inquisitive hands
so I can let these wings unfold and dry
so I can leap into that startling void.

I hope I will soar. I hope I will sing.
I hope I will meet up with other cicadas,
our wings a crackling testament to our joy.

Dream of Extraordinary Ease

Sometimes there's utter collapse
neither can move
and things that had disappeared
reappear
the flickering blue television light
arguments gun fights car chases

the dog groans and stretches
the furnace kicks on
across the skin a small frostiness
and we pull up the covers

You reach for my hand
or maybe I reach for yours
Somewhere in the world
our grown children are living
On weekends they call—

Maybe this is our american dream
a dream of extraordinary ease
where love finds its expression
in the everyday way you smile at me
when I say something amusing
or when you know the answer to my puzzlement
or can reach the highest shelf
the way this flush of desire
leaves me grounded here on earth
my heart rushing toward you

Roadside Encounter

I

Another cardboard box, split at the sides,
has toppled off the back of a pick-up truck—
or is it a bag of leaves tied in haste?
The animal-shaped spill lifts its jaw—
the angled box carving to a backbone,
the entrails like styrofoam peanuts
coiling pale and strangled.

II

Nearing, I see its deer shape, unmistakable,
I lower the sun visor,
fiddle with the radio,
look to the left (surely there's something else),
but my eyes drag back to the scene,
where the deer has elongated,
as she might have done yesterday,
after gathering herself for the leap.
My foot eases up as I crane for a closer look,
see where metal met flesh,
a chest wound, the jaw thrown back
like a saint's agony, reaching toward the
shoulder of the road,
toward something watching in the brush.

III

Someone has veered across her—
the carcass—leaving tire marks
bold as the sign of a cross.
Crawling by, I see that other life has descended.
Not only the grackles that circle the air,
but their crawling cousins,
burrowing into niches
cold as the outdoors—
even their furious squirming can't warm this place.

IV

My eyes skim over the dried husk,
flattened as leather—
a saddle seen better days,
old car seat from a luxury model,
shoes, boots, piles of them,
stretched out tongue to tongue,
lascivious as a drunken cobbler
rising out of the past
to take what's his,
material for patching,
something worth keeping.

V

My tire blows just beyond and I pull over,
lean against my car, as if it doesn't bother me
that grackles cross her flank,
their tails lifted, like waitresses
in short skirts reaching for the floor.
I shoo them away—"nasty things"—
now closer than I've ever been,
then closer, the only tool I could find in hand—
the tire gauge like a physician's pointer, lifting the hide.
Inside, things have quieted down:
colors decoded into meaningless statements.

VI

The next morning, mended, my car hurtles past.
I almost forget to look, then in the last moment
I do. I owe it to her,
to acknowledge our short history,
what she meant to me in those moments
that fit into the day so neatly,
there, gone, a moment's puzzler,
then the clarity of everyday business.
Her ribs arc like a big cat's swipe,
claws extended for maximum purchase,
or like the grand entrance to a public domain,
a sculpture garden, a place of prayer,
the bones domed as fingers, exquisite,
swirling with bits of cosmic gravel and soot.

VII

Another day.
She's finally gone, delivered into the dump truck
just before I crest the hill.
I see the man throw a shovel into the back,
then climb in the passenger's side.
I slow down to let them enter the lane,
I want them to go first, I want to follow.
Good workers, they've left nothing to imagination,
only this knowledge:
behind that swinging gate, now latched,
a skeleton un-enamored of flesh
emits what's left of the sun
a faint heat, for sure,
almost enough to see, rising.

Far, Far Away, in Vilnius

A paper boat and an empty carton of juice
dangled from a bridge over the river.
Why, you asked, did someone do that?

I said, two children were playing
in the water with boats they had made,
and afterward they hung them out to dry.

Then, in the river, we saw
a stack of shapely rocks, then another, then many.
They looked dribbled from the sky, dabbles of brown paint—

why are the rocks piled just so, you asked, why?
In this city of churches, I said, pagans come to the water,
gripping the slick stones with their toes then hoisting them high.

And not only that, I say, here in the side streets of Vilnius
doorways too small to step through
unless you're an elf or a child or an old couple stooped over.

I miss my home, I tell you, which is why I'm sad.
Is it a big missing, you ask—no, it's a little one, like a notch
on one of these padlocks attached to this bridge by people in love.

We lift and turn them and they settle with a clink above the water,
and then I ask if you have a lock for us, knowing you don't—
our just discovering them like that, on the way to someplace else.

Confession

I arrive early, hands jangling pieces
from another game of Monopoly
I couldn't bear to finish. I pull them out, familiar
as my failings, and line them up on the ledge
on my side of the confessional. Leading the way,
no surprise, the silver Scottie noses into places
he has no business going—

Next, the iron's blunt chin and that starchy frown . . .
Behind the screen, you clear your throat.
Hold on, I say, I think we're getting somewhere—

Look, the sports car has screeched to a halt,
sneering at the little plow when it pulls up
ready to argue, some dirty little secret
about who does the real work
and who spends half a day covering his tracks.

You clear your throat again. It's ten o'clock in the morning
and I've been moving pieces around for thirty minutes.
Things are heating up as the line of penitents reaches
the outer door, or maybe they're just sightseers
tapping their hymnals against the backs of pews.
I say, maybe we should talk later, perhaps this evening

when the lilacs have closed and the crickets
begin their leg-rubbing—or do they go at it all day long?

Could we stroll around the cemetery where the old nuns
swing their rosaries, chanting in syllables so low
you'd think it was rocks in the creek tumbling toward the rapids—
I hear it takes one pebble seven years to make its way from the bridge
at the big clock to the bend outside the window there,

where the red Jesus has lifted his hammer and stands ready
to let it fall into a pile of gold and blue lumber. I always liked
that window best, you know, the one where he's working
with his hands not raising them over the children's heads
or lowering them to someone's feet, where he's looking up
as if someone's just called him to dinner, or he's just
remembered something more urgent he needs to do.

Someone Else's Offspring

At night I hear the fluttering of the bird,
some starling's darling trapped
after the gables were repaired last week.
The wings rap at the wire mesh
and then begin their whispering.

I crawl out my window,
climb up to the neighbor's balcony
(who are traveling in some godforsaken place)
then shimmy up the brownstone
and flash a light into the quiet darkness
behind the silver grille.

I want to free the tyke but the landlord refuses
to answer the phone,
and all day long the ventilator fan pulls
feathers and dust and slivers of insulation
and shoots them into the dew-starved air . . .

Teeth gripping the screwdriver I have for repairs
and inserting batteries into your childhood toys,
I make a second trip, knees hugging and sinews twisting
as my hand reaches beyond what's natural
and unhinges a corner of the wire cover.

The hole admits my fingertips—
like creatures that have crossed the line into abomination

they writhe at the edge of the starling's night.
I cough up the bit of lettuce, rice patty, raw ground beef
I've been carrying under my tongue and glue it
to the screwdriver's flat edge,

then pierce the cross-hairs with a stab
and leave it, along with *something* more substantial,
some *words* to get the poor fellow through the night.

I grip the wall. I chirp.

The Shape and Size of Things

They say that a heart is the size of a fist.
And that a blue whale's tongue weighs
as much as an elephant.

What does that tell us about the elephant?
Or the whale? They are big.
They belong in different places.
Would the glass remain half-full if a fist
ripped out the heart and settled
into that slippery absence?

A fist gnarled with rage, hungry for love,
might think that a ball of flesh and bone
could take up residence in this home,
without causing a stir—

How could it know, floundering
at the end of an arm, shaking at the skies,
zounds! zounds! balled against the eyes,
burrowing into someone else's flesh,
or clutching the pillow from the depth of sleep . . .

I want to whisper to the fist:
mention the marrow
the affinity of bone and liquid,
then ask, Is there room at the inn for me?

After

I

A disarray of thoughts
in the fall-touched hills behind our house:
they say the brightest colors need
sunny days cool nights no rain.

Misty and gray it is, then,
a thin shawl warm enough—
thoughts too myriad to distinguish
among the browns and golds

their lingering bouquet of tannic and amino
like a warning from beyond the hills,
breath from another world.

II

In the basin, hardy mums don't grow,
water stands long
bullfrogs bellow
and snapping turtles lie mute, then leave.

We tried dredging it, but the water
came back
seeping like a tobacco stain
across the struggling green.

We tried plugging it, but the leak
sucked the concrete blocks
and sealed the spot with a pucker.

In the basin, all things settle.
Only the water remains, bracken and mirrored.
In the world below, our attempts
bump and drop through channels like veins.

III
I lift these hands, unconditioned
to the absence of you—
what is this slow dance
and why do I offer my arms to it?

Some things have left and that's the problem—
strange pronunciations
of familiar places.
Hills, a low spot, seasons, a home,
nouns that verbs like to hover over

like hands, maybe, touching in the night
or like space when there's no more sinking
left to do.

Kodiak Ghazal

At dusk, the Kodiak reaches a heavy paw into the rushing stream—
the salmon a shower of gold and light against the darkening stream.

I see them rimmed in white, a snapshot from a dream, though sometimes
the bear looks up at me and then my heart is a roar that silences the stream.

Is she the Other or do I see myself hungry and full of purpose
pulling something from its known world, now a blooded stream?

She locks me with her stare, a whuffing at her curling lips, nose high,
body rocking as she rises above her hind legs, water streaming.

The eyes are ancient, close-set and keen for preying, body hot
and reeking of musk and earth and fish from that mountain stream.

Last night I felt the water slip along my sides, inhaled it and let it out,
racing reflections through a sun- and shade-splattered stream.

And tonight I had to choose between the sound of gasping and the raking
at my heart, bear them both or surrender to the spirit stream.

Two White Pigeons

On this gray day when the May sun
has no burn left to dry the wind,

we return from our walk through
the monastery fields and woods

hungry for hot soup and gazing.
The dark green pond stretches

from window to window of this
rental cottage in the country

where we have retreated
from the gray hovering life

we know. Redwing blackbirds cut
the air and settle in the branches

of a tree that has died and stands
waiting—or savoring—its own

end of story. The shallow waters
ripple in the wind or the wake

of gray geese who paddle to the shores
and dive, but don't die, like the old song,

a-standing on their heads—and how I miss
that old song about Aunt Rhody's gray goose,

a song too sad to bear when I was a girl
who didn't see what was so dangerous

about standing on your head or why someone
would put it all down like that, in a song.

Memory wavers like a shadow, as two
snowy egrets land near the far shore

and begin their long-necked
wading, so intent on subtle movement

they are not startled by the blaze of two
white pigeons that fly out of blue clarity

and stop my breathing, if not my heart—three times
circling the pond in breathless nips and tucks,

stitching up the terrible rending
that has pulled our lives apart.

Whisper

Last night I dreamed
my boys were fighting.
That was long ago, and yet
they are ten or eleven again,
and one of them has hit or twisted
some part of the other's body
so that he is curved into the wall.

A blade sudden as a ray of light
cuts heart-deep, and my own voice
rushes at me from across the room:
"I can't do this anymore!"

They disappear, the boys—
it's the alone that tells you
no one is coming—
walls and ceiling receding fast.

What is it you can't do anymore—
stand by watching, hands dangling
or cupped and asking to be filled?

I reach across the rocking floor
seeking what it is that holds me here—
my dog's soft ears,
her warm scent of a cared for animal,
the sweat that leaves

gray trails behind my child's child's knees—
yes, these are the things I'll miss.

And you? What will you miss?
Tell me. I'm in no hurry
and am learning to listen underneath
when someone says
it doesn't matter and all is well.

tree forms

Bulky Thing

I thought they would hold,
but you all slipped through
one by one

what remains,
a bulky shape and heavy.

If these limbs could unbend
they'd set the record straight:

some childhood pain turned wood
then petrified

some more recent thing, perhaps
made up of parts of you,
what was too removed to see

too shadowy to uproot.

Camping on Greys River, Bridger Tetons

Why do they do it?
Scratching the aspens this way . . .

I feel them watching from the sun-lit copse
as my fingers trace their four vertical scars—
more animal than others,
dangerous if fed.

That night, it was cold, the river current
paused a moment, opened a pocket

of silence in the rushing
conversation with brown stones.

I felt the throb of the tent cords
when the body assaulted them
and heard the *shoosh*
of fur against nylon.

I did not yell "Go!"
but curled around the vital organs
and waited for the cuff that would send me
spinning through the zippered door—
even lifted my face to the frosty air
and sought its hot, hungry breath
stinking of rot and musk and dark.

Why the dream of rushing into terror?

As though I welcomed
a final "this is it"
wanted to expose my belly

surrender, my self
to the other self.

Aspen Hieroglyphs

Once below the surface, now

they rise
darkening the white skin,

like paths of a mole—even,
when you run your fingers over me.

These bruises beyond recall,
incidental wallops like the @ sign,
jagged lines, pursed lips of tissue—

So transparent, you say,
this writing on the skin,
what do you expect me to say—

In the dip between my collarbones
where you used to place your tongue,
a pool is forming—

Dip a finger there and touch your brow.

Pando

In Utah is a stand of Aspen, the visible
sign of a vast underground organism,
perhaps the largest in the world.

Your charcoal eyes are hooded
as though you had glimpsed Eternity

or the microbe that could bring down
what nothing larger-than exists.

Is this green plane we share a mirror
for your slender whitebark fingers

or does your secret self speak its vast
knowledge in whispers,

pushing through earth and debris,
to all those subterranean creatures—

while above your public self
just *ooohs* and *aaahs*, and bends

like stricken passersby,
with the wind?

On Disappointment

If you feel gutted, it may be too late
to take heed.

Were you dozing when you fell,
never heard the warning sounds?

You must see the point
of turning it all into something else:

the massive tree on its back,
you, dissected and exposed.

Cells remember and ashes rise,
we dine on the remains of others.

When I Fall

When I fall, I'd like it to be
in a very clear lake
at the top of a mountain.

I'd like to know that I will see
the mounting fuzziness of moss
and beneath, the hard calcium
of other elements

that fishes dart beneath me
in the sun, and above, the brilliant stars
pulse in harmony.

I'd like to fall with a splash
and ripples that hit the shores and come
back to me, saying

yes, it's there.

When I fall, I'd like to know it's near home,
that my roots, even exposed
are familiar
if not exactly what they were before.

Make it green with a hint of blue,
and me, bleached of all color

just a path, narrow and tentative
for some tiny creature

seeking the other side.

Who Listens to an Old Woman?

I'm the mad one
living out my days at the edge of the village
fussing about with herbs (likely worse)
or holed up in an attic someplace
sorting through my bristlecone needles

Who listens to me?
I set my knees in rock
and twist until I see the path
I took, those centuries long

Come hither, my pretty, as I unfurl myself
and cast a shadow that arches over you—
there, with that doubt you feel
in the twinge of spine and air,
in your sweetly curled ears and pierced lobes

in the sleepless night when you
bang your knee and knuckle
against the dark—

Who wants to hear the Queen's "when I was a girl," after all?
It's like seeing the slender legs slipping
out of a warty trunk,
the rosebud inside brash tubers
too knotty to be whittled away,

or feeling the throb of a nascent pulse
inside your most delicate of places.

It's knowing that you can't slip my embrace
once you let my piney scent drill down,
that what you dreamt one
quiescent dawn when
your sleeping self let go for just a moment too long
and heard my lullaby crooned, for you—
was in fact no dream,
was a branch (olive or thorned)
perhaps a hand.

Come hither, my pretty,
remember the mirror,
and listen to an old woman

I'll explain why your dreams no longer invite you to fly.

Write My Back

This child pleads, "Write my back!"
and tells me what I've written,
"Erase it and do another word!"
Her slender tablet barely contains
her anticipation as my fingers
climb the delicate ladder.

She is our volcano of joy
overrunning corners of the room
where she can go higher than the air or fall.

Will she see herself just tolerated,
and become someone always trying harder?
Will our faces tell her
she is magnificent beyond belief
and she has become a shallow stream?

Or will she stay the radiant light we know today?

The back is no means to another end,
something left unsaid, not a wall—
is a reminder of how the landscape
holds the sky.

It's not so much turning your back
on what's there,

as deciding what to let in.

Sitting at My Uncle's Window

At first you find it tiresome:
what's there but a gravel alley,
three garages, their doors in trim, ajar,
a lawn, two white plastic chairs
a flag lifting and folding
from its pole in the tree?

I've seen a picture where this stunted thing
blossomed a broad Derby hat with little white flowers,
but now, the tree's pruned way back,
a stiff man—almost Jesus—caught *in medias res*
his arms raised, a yellow
thermometer like a badge on his chest,
flagpole spearing his back.
His head, shaved, tilts
slightly to the left and at his feet,
red and blue leashes wrap tight
where the dogs stopped.

You can watch the neighbors and muse
with the old man why it is
they've stacked eight drawers
on their concrete slab
yet only a four-drawer cabinet.

You can watch the scudding gray
and wonder, will it rain?

Or count the pigeons, ravens,
blue jay, wrens, the darting chickadee,
and wonder why there are
so few robins this year.

Perhaps what you really want to know
is how this confluence occurred:

the twigless lawn, its clean-cut grass
the old man with his deep gaze
sitting in one of the white chairs,
whiskey in hand . . .

Visits are rare, though the town asks after him,
his daughter cooks and cleans for him,
trims his beard,
prods him into his daily walk,
his arms stretched low to steady his gait
fingers spread, almost a bird—

You might wonder what goes on in the mind
of a quiet man, at eighty-seven. Though he doesn't hear
so well, you might get his attention. He'll lean in.

  "Do you like the way the flag's tied up?"

His answer comes so slow
you think he has forgotten
or doesn't like the question—then,
"Did I like the blackbird pie?"

The sun breaks through for a moment
and I lean across the sill.
The bald tree's medal has slipped
a star is seceding from the other forty-nine,
a sweat bee lands on the screen
then loops the air like a shoestring
tied with an impatient drone

two pigeons shuffle and shamble

—they need eyes on the sides of their heads
so they can see the predators coming.

Bad Habits

Who can resist the raven,
solitary or in gangs?

Is it their bulky size, their coal-dust dinginess,
those crabby voices they use with each other,
beady eyes and sharp hooked beak,
or the bullying of sweet-singing birds?

Ravens are habits I've endured:
beard hairs on toilet seats
girls who suck the ends of their hair
smelly socks on lampshades . . .

They are the fears I harbor:
this innate shallowness apparent to all
but the equally superficial,
the dream where you my love have died
and then the awful waking . . .

All of them shim-feathered and beady-eyed,
breathing through hard-and-fast nostrils.

I watch the literal referents
do reconnaissance on a stand of old pines
circle slender limbs with their long twiggy feet.
I hear the grand old trees admonishing the younger ones,
"What do you accomplish shivering and rustling like that?

You can't just shake your shoulders and be rid of them.
You have to get Buddhist with them,
let the wind move in,
savor it like a groan,
tuck it under the branch where they wait,
shitting down your spine—
meanwhile stand up straight,
and when the moment is right (only then)
lean back and *zing* them to a feathery tomorrow.

They'll be back."

The Story They Tell Is Our Story

Two trees started green and leaned in slow—
took their lifetime to become this arch.
They seem an old couple we might know,
their lives now stories their bodies tell.

Consider the one on the left,
see how it has twisted, reaching
for the other until forced away—
by war or peace, the demands of work
—and yet, look!

See it reach a limb across the divide
(though the span is shy).
Like you, I think, reaching across
the space between us:
Were the children done then?
Was work the way you wanted it,
or gone beyond what you had to offer?
Why didn't I lean harder then,
and when was it clear
my slow arch was toward you?

Couldn't you have pushed that limb,
acknowledge that I, inclining always to the left
was steady as the seasons?

It was that second reach, wasn't it,
that stripped us down, said
this, or nothing—

It was evident then, when first these trees—
one smooth and pointed but how slow!
one pocked and twisting—
began the spinal dance that ever and a day

pulls us in. Love it is, then,
and all that baggage we strip away.

There's always a story, theirs or ours:
I hear you say, take me as I am, love,
bare and bristly,
you have only and always been the one.

These Things Left Behind

Call it unkempt, this hanging moss in a pine
still damp from last month's flooding of the Colorado—
here, at its source, miles before the damming.

Left by wind and rain it joined the pine,
yet is not the pine.

Names like *Usnea* and *Alectoria*
don't tell us much about these pendula in green,
like Spanish moss misplaced—strangely
draping, lacy, storied.

Back in Kentucky, brown walnut leaves exhale
their former green and the wind sniffs it up,
while yellowed cousins spoon the air—

grounded but adding to the stew
mown grass froths like the receding brine
of waves along another shore.

See how a toad, true *Bufonidae*, paused and went no further,
his forearms tucked under,
his head bowed . . . such a prayerful silence—
none of his brethren to clean up after,
nor even a passer-by to toe the spirit-emptied casing. . . .

There are other ways to mark
the passage of time
than appointments, deadlines,
clean-up, the coffin,

and more to substrate than stratagem
more to lawn and pavement
than the edge that separates them.

Things get left behind, witness
our habits of noticing.

Oak Tree at the Window

I want to be the oak tree at my window
strong in the center, many-branched
and reaching in every direction

a place where the wind can tell
it's making an impression

transforming atoms with my breath
speaking H_2O

joy becomes sadness becomes joy
my skin reaches over
blessings and mistakes

sculpting new shapes

Intrusion

In early morning
        the room is dark—
                air is charged
                      by morning about to erupt
              Beyond the window frame
        the branchy fingers
of the old box elder knuckle under.

Amorphous lines harden
        in the light-frosted cold,
                while the killdeer scream
                      from the fields and then alight.
                Crabbing in the branches
        they knock their obsession
against the hollow trunk.

Gray then pink the air quickens
        seducing the tree
                out of darkness.
                      They sing in another register now
                of the soft purple of early morning snow
        and an acquiescent dawn
caroling *amazing*.

The Hole

I see the rugged opening in the upright trunk
(blaze of white) and make my way,
slipping on rock and moss
and kneel before it.
My fingers read the fluted rim—
I know this hole, but how?
I have to kneel to look through.

It's the reversible sleeve of negative space,
Freud's delirious dark continent,
a doorway to enchantment.

It's a brazen slash across the throat or gut
that leaves you speechless
your eyes saying
I meant to call home,
wanted another chance,
am thinking of you . . .

a sacred portal between this world and
this same world made better,
where we might find happiness at last.

It's the cesarean with the Other gone,

or what would happen
if the implied line between our right and left split
and all that belongs *in* came rushing *out* . . .

a place where your fingers
walk the secret folds and swells and ridges,
where I invite you wholly in.

It's where I place things and then forget
I've put them there or that this place
that holds my belongings even exists—
forgetfulness itself.

It was always sick, that spot,
and we only learned after, when
it popped like a cork.

It's the place our paths diverge
an unbridgeable fissure
the hiatus of truth
a reminder all our lives that
we have hurt ourselves most grievously
and yet here we are . . .

It's old age divulging secrets—what
point to hold them anymore?

A metaphor for wisdom, the *almost*, the *if*.

Escape for winds that shake the canyon
where the cosmic scream (or whistle),
sounds—put your ear there

and god will whisper to you.

Heart of the Matter

The bark on my oak tree is not a study in brown.
Lichen has curved around the eastern sides
and the sun has just caught hold of a bare patch,
pale gray and smooth as a face and edging into moss,
moss that grips the shadow parts like a hand—
while neighboring shavings hang by a thread.

Up close, don't you suppose the tiny leaves
are fragile against the heavy boot? My head
darkens the gray and sends a large brown ant
into a hole, though it emerges right away
and jogs over to my hand, not fearful after all—
what of the occasional shadow overhead?

Pale green clusters of seed-bearers hang
like ornaments, infused with yellow. Birds
fly through the branches on roads of air,
a dozen different conversations, perhaps
about mating or what neighborhood to choose,
now that the old one's falling apart.

My tree is full of stories, how life goes on
will not be stayed, even by the grossest
human acts . . . will grow against all odds
and provide shade and oxygen and shelter,
I want to believe! I want to enter the tree,
put my fingertips against that natural armor

and watch as the very tips—my own exo-
expression—begin their entry, first the cambium,
that watery layer with a roar so loud my cries
surrender to the open mouth of silence—
then my spine fills with tubes of xylem,
and my feet leave ground behind as I wave

one last farewell to the house where I used to live.
Phloem has charged me with what I must do.
I feel the outer reaches pulling at my fingertips,
the knock of my knees against the lower branches, and
something inside me pulsing toward the inner ring,
dark purple heartwood, death at the center.

I live now in the heart of the matter, where the road
between now and then has opened into possible.
See my son lower his weight on the grown-up swing
where he can watch his daughter swing on hers. See
me release a prayer into his folded hands, something
he can twirl by the stem, the resin a golden smudge.

the casey poems

Blessed by the Dalai Lama

The cross is cool this morning
as I lean forward and it falls
against my left breast.
I will warm it there
the pretty silver T on a red string
blessed by the Dalai Lama.

We found it where you slept one night
when you must have turned and pulled
the silver chain until it snapped.

I try to see you as you must have looked
the night we lost you,
the moments it took for the bullet to enter
your shoulder and ricochet off your rib
and pierce your lung and heart and lodge against your rib.

Such a great spiritual leader—surely
his blessed string could have entered you,
could have retraced the path of anger
could have threaded its way
back, back, back
and closed the unnecessary hole
could have pulled the metallic smell of absence out.

Cyan

Though we will never meet, I have come to love a man named Houchins, the one who tried to bring our youngest back. Because the business of dying must travel from desk to desk, it takes two months for his report to reach us. I see him in the act, hunched over a clipboard beneath the red screaming of the ambulance as it tore through the night. For five pages, his hand is firm, and the print is dark, no smudges or broken nibs, despite the hills and potholes.

And yet his phrases are foreign road signs in familiar terrain—pupils fixed, BVM employed, ETCO2, the sound of air escaping lungs above the sirens, IO/IV, swelling chest, NSS, and the young man's skin giving over to cyan as the flush of blood withdrew.

Outside, the winter landscape is uncertain about the strip of blue on the horizon. Gray presses down, washing out the tones that allow us to get away with calling it blue, even when it has weakened to a memory.

The night we read the report, I dreamt they laid our boy on a table and left me alone to study his face—the returning pink that didn't belong, the tear that escaped his eye and rolled down his cheek. I helped him sit and strained to understand the language already turned against him— words knocking in his throat like tumbling boulders and his urgency a rushing flood. I spoke the only levee I knew to slow him down, "How I loved you, *loved*!" each word a sandbag. He hesitated, "Did you?" and then understanding broke across his brow: "I know you did."

The memory of his arms still cresting my shoulders, I lift the curtains and note the flush of morning and the black arms of the oak, each one capped with white and muffling what happens when one world gives way to the other.

Imperative

I

You came home from a church retreat
where kids make crosses out of bamboo strips
or paper plate masks,
wind socks or bookmarks—
but this time a necklace of beads
black and white on a red string:
don't forget about me.

Were you rephrasing Christ's request
or spelling out a sweet indictment,
the imperative about yourself and not God's son?
In all the falderal of work and life,
not now, go play, stop hanging on me,
still, I never forgot!

II

What were you thinking, the night you died,
driving to a place so clearly marked
by fear and degradation and rushing
toward the lowest circles of hell?

If you had known of its hidden arsenal
of guns and compound bows,
flak jackets, MREs, and sawed off shot-guns,
stacked so thick the detectives could barely move—
would you have hesitated?

What were you thinking when you pulled away?
Did you roll down your window to shout one last
invective? Did he burst out of the house like a cowboy
through swinging barroom doors?
Or slink, like Rambo, around the
auto graveyard that circled the shack like a noose?

III

I hold a grape and close my fingers
until the skin retracts and the slippery globe
falls quivering into my hand—
slender veins encircle it and thread all through,

My palm is wet with sweetness,
the thick casing still between my fingers.
I prod the perfect sphere into its vulnerable hole
where a stem once gave the sac shape.
Do I have it right, your imperative?
Or were you lamenting a deed already done:
forgot about me.

Madmen seek no proof of beauty
but cower in the darkness of their shredded hearts,
and scrape their shadows across the way,
enduring their suspended sentence,
perhaps even since they were children,
their sunken voices garbling
have you forgotten me?

Hydrostatic Shock

Today we are putting the pieces together. Yesterday, we had the news. Tomorrow, and tomorrow, we'll have the ever-crashing waves. But today we learn about calibers and hydrostatic shock.

A .40 caliber does what .22s fail to do. Faster and more penetrating, .22s pass through, leaving the enemy alive. A .40 caliber lopes along and flattens a little, when meeting something hard, like bone. Dreamed of in 1990 by the highly successful arms developers Smith & Wesson, the .40 caliber travels 1,000 feet or so per second.

You can't see that kind of velocity, but you can wonder at how quickly it slows, knowing that shoulder to farthest rib in a young man is only a matter of inches. Compared to manlier missiles, the .40 was laughable—dubbed Short & Wimpy and Slow & Weak. Yet the .40 caliber gains penetration and gives up only speed . . .

Once it takes its Sunday stroll through soft tissue, pressures develop. They measure these in thousands of atmospheres, which feels about right, and categorize them in threes, like the Big Bang, linear: First, sharp pulses where the surface is struck. Then, whole regions to the front and sides of the moving missile. And third, low maybe quieter changes in the cavity behind it. Experts disagree, but this appears plausible.

Some shock won't kill, but in liquid-filled tissue, such as lungs and heart, destruction reaches far beyond the path of the rimless straight casing and its 32,000 pounds (give or take) per square inch.

One man likes it because "Penetration crushes more tissue, bone, and hopefully an artery," while this one dispenses with hope: "Less energy, more *momentum*, bigger hole." We find it interesting that .40 caliber paintballs fit any .40 caliber blowgun.

Tomorrow we may want to learn more—but today we know enough: how a nanosecond can hold a swirling cosmos of befores and durings and afters; and how their ballistics got one thing right: there is a cavity involved.

The Tree You Come Home To

In the story I used to read to you
about the runaway bunny,
Mother Rabbit is always the very thing it takes
to bring her bunny home.

A page hangs in a poster frame on your wall—
"If you become a bird and fly away from me,
I'll be the tree you come home to."

Now that you have said, "I will die and
leave this earth and you behind,"
Mother Rabbit just wags her carrot
and I don't know what shape
I can pour myself into
that can possibly bring you home—

Shall I become a wisp of light and scent
so you will recognize the angel who embraces you?

If I become the place where your shadow feet
can still leave an impression,
would you know me as the path you take
to find yourself at god's feet?

Beside the shivers of worm trails
and carcasses of insects,
I reach inside and grasp the place that weeps,

so you will know

in the way that spirits know

the weight is yours, is mine.

Things That Are Hot and Cold

the way you used to blow
one day a sulking cobra
the next, a ray lifting the hooded eye
and a smile easing the wariest of hearts

fingers stiffening around a cigarette
as December flattens the flame of a candle
I've placed on the patio railing

your forehead where I pressed my lips
your purpled lips and eyelids fastened shut
the room where we stood holding hands
and your father cried,
sweet jesus what have they done to you—

emptiness, what you knew of death on earth
fear when you saw a demon snarling
in the mirror . . . and *crack*!
the underworld came boiling to the surface

stumbling from the room in hopes that ignoring you
as you screamed in my face
how much you hated me
would prove to you that love endures . . .

your low voice mumbling "love you"
the spill of blood sluicing between organs
my fingers when the cigarette goes out

Minor Chord

If I could write a minor chord, it would begin
with a gesture I know well, a nod or touch,
a particular lilt in the gait, the manner
of shoulders held just so, and then

the nod would be too bright
the touch a little heavier than quite right,
the familiar lope would catch
like a fingernail between the thirds and fifths

and shoulders that carry their weight
with a soft apology would stride
too widely off the canvas
and pull the colors to the side

If I could sing or paint a wounded child
the eyes' upward appeal would sound a wail
and the bloodied brow still seep
though it's hours since I put the brushes away,

voices would creep through the muted landscape
like a conversation from another room
and the rocky ledge where god might reach a hand
crumble and begin to slip away

the moment would rise up when corded muscles
mutate and the song in the throat

find passage in the haunted field
where winter flowers clamor for the sun

Twenty-One Tomorrow

Snow covers the branches of the oak
and needles of the cedar. Flakes
like dimes sift through the open spaces
and rise along corridors of light.
The sky, white as the snow itself, says
all is chill, all day long
and the wind turns vertical on its side.

Tomorrow our son would have been twenty-one.
We might have taken him out.
Or said (as we did every year), "Any wisdom
you can share from your first twenty-one?"
For certain, we'd have known that
rubbing his head and squeezing his shoulder
were ours for the taking.

And so I ask, you with your sighs and drifting shrugs,
in your patient merging of the weightless and the profound,
could you help me reach him—some light touch, cool
on his cheek or forearm, where
all is not chill or the night gone?

Memento Mori

I knew the feel of your head in my hands, your body tucked in the
bowl my elbows made. By nine your canines completed your smile,
and by fourteen, we turned and walked away when you pulled off your
dirty socks.

Look behind you, remember that you are but a man, said the slave
trailing the emperor during the flush of victory, and 2,000 years later
the town clock echoes *vulnerant omnes, ultima necat*, they all wound,
and the last kills. Is it true, as Montaigne said, that the one who learns
how to die unlearns how to be a slave? When angels snuff candles
do they ache with memories, or are they merely asking us to forget
the world and think on how it slips away? Despise the flesh, its mess
of blood, bone, and bowels, its tangle of nerves, veins, arteries—and
liberate the divine soul.

How grateful we were when Dr. Gupta took a bit of bone from your
hip and patched your broken wrist, a nearby artery providing the drink.
We have a picture of you—across your heart the repaired arm rests.

Krsa the grieving mother went to the Buddha for help. *Take away my
pain*, she said, but instead he sent her on a quest for mustard seeds and
the admonition to accept them only if the giver had never lost anyone.
She carried her dead baby in her arms. They pitied her but she could
not take their mustard seeds. This one had lost a daughter, that one a
father, here an uncle, every step along the way a son, mother, sister,
friend. Realizing the community of grief, her sorrow abated—perhaps
enough to relinquish the corpse in her arms.

I've not thought about your kidney or spleen, bowels, intestines, shit, or phlegm, but loved the heart of you, and the breath. Searching this divine marrow, I'd recognize it all—if angels retain such things, and I could not despise any of it.

We die alone. We grieve alone. It isn't true that we grieve and die alone. It could be rosemary or thyme as well as mustard seeds that I would withhold to share if she came knocking at my door.

Rogue Tongue

What owe I the stranger's curiosity,
and yet—I oblige! I oblige!
spanning the public story
and what only we who love you know
of the night your life was stolen.

Against a larger silence,
my mouth is a trigger-happy gate
for words splashing down the sluice.

They dance, they catch the light, they lie.

Within the private silence,
I breathe into the cathedral of my hands
with their arches of bone and flesh,
ivory walls clatter shut around roof and palate
and the rogue tongue spins out its soft lament:

Spirit child, will you speak to me?
Are you truly free of pain,
or does the blueness linger there as well
like the clothing of a sacred memory?

If your answer's yes,
or if it's no . . . or if you have no answer,
go then to the lonely place—
I will meet you there.

Ghazal, by a Thread

Love is a thread that will not break, though in this gray life
it surely must, bearing as it does, so much—yours, theirs, my life

Last night I walked a star-crazed night, then sat on the old swing
until the bare branches glittered, morse-coding a splintered life

In utter stillness sometimes, I hear a whispering, things not living, spirits
piercing the plane that separates us—though not you, silent from life . . .

So new to their world—are you seeking a way through, some breach?
I search the edge of every odd-shaped thing—scrap of life—

and ask, What on earth is the matter? What does it mean to be the thing
that ended next to you? What difference are you to your own life?

The silhouette I've made for myself, chalking up scorn for this
or that, is blurring and the lines redrawing—it seems the life

I've called my own is but an echo of someone else, someone
who can only be heard—or found—if she lets go of that life

sloughing off the skin and bearing the rawness, pulling
hand over hand and gathering the lines of this deep-shadowed life.

The Weight of a Human Heart

If you could trace this line in the air, you'd hear it rise and fall like shore-borne waves, swelling, breaking, gathering for more. At the far end, you'd watch as they lost teeth and broke arms and cracked open their heads on corners of tables and tiled steps and splashed in gray bath water at the end of the day. You'd see them twist one another's arms and then request stories about stuffed animals that come alive in the dark, and in the end bottle up the early years, cork and shelve them.

You notice the mundane bleeding into the significant: how they shrugged their shoulders over trails of socks and shoes or dirty dishes—and then moved out, except for the youngest, who wanted to, promises riding the hot air, till they finally cooled and then settled, peaceable like, and anyway he didn't mean like this, and oh that the voice lingering still might be more than the wake of his passing loud as when he strode through the door calling "Mom, guess what, Mom?" any breeze carrying the smell of him and the weight.

He carried two dimes and a penny, on his left wrist wore a green friendship bracelet. The doctors mark it all: the right arm's tattoo of Jesus' head, bent, hands carrying a wooden cross, the left arm with his daughter's face accented by red roses, her little hand folded under her chin. They seek to know how X compares to Y, seem relieved that the lungs preserved their fine lacy architecture, that there was nothing remarkable about the intestines, and that toxicology was negative. They appreciate a body true to itself.

Theirs is a numbers story: how the lungs weighed four hundred-forty grams, and the palpable bullet lodged nine inches left of midline and fifty-three inches from the left heel, having blazed its path from the right shoulder, a downhill slope, thirty-to-thirty-five degree deviations. A story of contrasts. How devastating lacerations of lungs and thoracic aorta can leave untouched the adrenal gland's smooth yellow outer cortical rims overlying zones of deeper brown cortical and gray medullary substances, how a body's internal landscape tells of liquid harmony, where mucosa falls like drapery in longitudinal folds and walls are smooth and glistening. You couldn't find a more perfect container for his three hundred-thirty-gram heart, even when yours has tipped the scale, even when the landscape has darkened and the waves rise and fall in silence and the story you tell begins and ends *once upon a time.*

Architecture of Loss

I

A clear bell, clapper worn
to a strip of leather,
still the brass shivers and
mourners set down their work and draw near.

II

Words blister off the page
and float through the open window,
catching in the branches or whirling toward the hills.
People swim by, their mouths wide, elbows cocked.
One dimensional they are stripped to the basics,
like paper dolls. They don't notice the air
has been brushed with a graying wash.

III

The doors slam shut on the night-time
river of sliding images as the boy rises,
brushing leaves and debris from his shoulders.
He looks up, a grin spreads slowly across his face . . .
but something gives him pause—is it in my reach
for him or a shadow on the vaulted ceiling?—
Oh, to stop that cellular movement of knowledge across
the eyes, nose, mouth drawing down—
What am I doing in your dream?

*There, there, my darling, come and let me hold you,
I'm sorry I'm sorry I'm sorry . . .*

IV

Matter condensed and carried *just inside*.
If I pull it out and show you, it will sit in the center
of my palm for a moment and then pull my hand
to the ground. You will kneel down as well, curious,
and then the earth will tremble and you will notice
that a crater has formed around us,
my palm and the thing I wanted to show you
there at the center, attached by an arm, a body.
You will scramble away, pulling yourself
branch by branch toward the crest, and wave
over your shoulder—I don't blame you
for your swift departure.

I look at the hand that holds the matter,
pulsing black on an open star.
Do I return it to the place, *just here*,
where the heart once stood its post,
or let the eclipsing rim pull me in?

I think of Christina in the Wyeth painting.
Turned away her face might be awash in tears
or lit with gratitude, her body grounded but light.
Maybe she is the darkened house on the hill
and the vast landscape of golds and browns
the loneliness that bids her *go on*.

Second Year

The first year the sword made its home
in the tight place between the atria of my heart.
Some days it seemed the point
had broken away and traveled
to my eyes so that the world fragmented
and shone more brightly.
At night my fingers could not dislodge the handle
and I dreamt of goblin's breath—
the fairy tale woods of malevolent
branches and roots all grown up now
and serious.
Faint lights pulsed in the darkness.
Other times the blade seemed
to have slid out of its silky red home
and then the place it left
longed for its return.

As snowflakes mount their second dance
in the oak tree's branches, one limb
still wearing its ragged skirt of brown—
I miss the way the edge made shapes
of the body's meat, drew Zs in the dark
where the light would creep,
or slid filet-like between the ribs
and opened them.

Something new takes shape
grows long as a river,
dragging across a land that falters
and then joins the heavy sweep of loss . . .
becomes a hunching thing
no longer in the river
but of the river and watching
as dreams thrust up their skinny arms
and fingers catch the light
before they sink into marshy sag.

There is no desire.
It doesn't want to eat the rest,
it just does.

Requiem of the Bristlecone Pine at Lake Haiyaha

With love for Casey and gratitude to Johannes Brahms

I

Blessed, it is said, are those who mourn.
What began in perfect symmetry and fell
from the sky on this rock
has left parity for the innocent—

When did the twist of pale green
so succulent you could have drunk it
begin to twist and ache into itself?
Perhaps immediately, when it thrust an elbow
from its seedy casing and rose to see what world
it had entered, finding walls of rock
that wanted surfaces to tell their own story, only.

I see the brown seedcap rise
above Chaos Creek, birthed there as well,
sweet *Pinus aristata* seeking the familiar,
unprepared for the wind that took its breath away.

Gasping, it would have dropped to its knees
would have thrust its limbs out
would have grasped at anything
even the sharp edge of pale lichen.

II

Leaves have fallen during the night
and rain comes over the hill,
waking then rocking me back to gray.

I hear the footsteps of soldiers marching.
I run to them and pull their faces to mine
my hands read their cheekbones,
Have you seen him? Is he with you?

Their skin is soft beneath the grimy stains
of filth and tears;
they will not be slowed,
blind and deaf to distant gunfire
they carry what they think they'll need
and leave nothing to mark their passing
but this clump of withered grass.

My fingers curl around the dried edges
and linger here, where a bud once showed its face,
and there, where a root once sought its depth.

III

I run it through my fingers,
this one gray strand that will not stay
among its kind.

I bequeath my body the memory of you.
We'll begin with the place I carried you,
here, a round taut bowl
dense with the fiber of your silences—

all you could not bear about yourself
we'll place in here.
I'll watch the mass grow large
with all that's left to be said or done.

My arms will swell and twist with the effort
of lifting you from the wreckage
and carrying you home those long miles.
They will cry out as Atlas did

and bring these knees to the ground.
They will crack the rock that still says no
but they will not hear no . . .

Here, my back becomes my side my front
there is no dividing me anymore,
I reach for you until the winds
have turned me full
and then it is I who turn the winds.

Here is the cavity that closes nightly
and wrenches open again by day—

Prometheus, cousin!
What fat-bundled bones
might trick Zeus now?

My ears grow large for the sound of footsteps
across the landing
but learn instead the disappointing scrabblings
of mice and the sleep-talking woodbeams
that hold it in by day
and groan the full night
of all that is not well
of shouts and threats and tears—

this is the haunting of wood.

IV

On a crisp morning when I was alone
the mist rose like a penitent's delivery.
The shaft of sunlight may have been
a shaft of sunlight only,
and the voices of angels may not have risen.

Someone said we should not project our feeling natures
onto the animal, vegetable, and mineral worlds
and endow them with more than they can bear.
But I think we are not so distinct—
the deeper meanings of love

direct our feet and our feet say
we will take you there.

The most honest of creatures,
a tree reaches for the root of things
and for the merest hint of light.
The bristlecone pine asks to tell its story
not just the skin nor only the form of it,
but the holes and densest boles
whorls and scars,
the piney fingers—especially these—
poised in the act of flinging
a clump of needles, something so like
the beginnings of joy.

V

Resting in this pocket of time
I open the spiral-ringed notebook
where you mixed history and math and wrote your heart:

> *What if the Prodigal Son stayed proud?*
> *A son drifted into himself and found death on earth.*
> *Emptiness.*
> *How did he return to life?*
> *Humbling himself.*

The pencil nub thickens and the words
pale and stretch into each other
so I have to hold the pages to the light:

> *I haven't been doing many things positive*
> *and I don't see things positively.*
> *I don't see things like other people.*
> *I just don't see.*

Virginia Woolf wrote palimpsests to protect from hungry eyes.
You would have liked the idea of writing over writing,
her vulnerability and her clever texts—

> *Writing seems to help, but I don't really share it.*
> *Not really shy but don't want to offend anyone.*
> *I can write a lot and get most of it out,*
> *but I'm not sure what "it" is.*

I stack the pages and study the palimpsest
of words and crisscrossed lines that rise
from when you scraped the sharpened point across your scars.

> *It might just be a little right now,*
> *but I feel a lot better.*
> *Starting to think more positively and not get upset as easily.*

It's not good to read what was written in secret
unless it's aloe you divine—
some truth you've ignored or overlooked
to lay across the damaged place.

VI

On the night he shoots and kills you
the semi-automatic's blunt nose extends his face and finger
and its open nostril flares.
Loud retorts echo from his craven heart,
and the whistling paths that sting the air
thicken into threads of rope.
Four spent casings
cry out as they hit the ground
as though emerging from a mouth.

Three shots slam into the tree beyond
where bark and fiber splinter,
sending a shock through the entire system,
down into the hairy tips of roots
that caress a waiting burial ground
and waken spirits who rise, rise, rise.
Some circle the place, while others
grab hold of passing cars.
Their tears are ancient and the dreams
they enter carry a new taste of rot
that will grow familiar and large with hunger.

He thought you were his for the taking
and those of us whose boy you really were
are swallowed by the cavern of the sky,
dream of falling
and wake to the shuddering of our bodies.

On such a night one comes to me
rolling out a carpet of crumbling leaves and dirt.
A breath is laid against my lips like a finger,
love and blessing trumpet through me,
your broad shoulders curve over me
and then you mouth the words you loved:
choose life.

VII

Blessed, it is said, are the dead.

Already your torments have lost their sting
and your good works follow you.

We speak of being better people
and set our timid feet upon the ground.

I begin to see that when peace enters
its succor will not pervade

that nothing will stay the loss of you except you
in your new form, moving and yet still.

I pull you close
the way I always pulled you close

and note again the sweetness and despair
that made you wise beyond your years.

We gave and took, you and I, and evermore
I fill my hands and lift them to you.

Drink. Then, let us go.

About the Author

Jane Olmsted's poems and stories have appeared in *Nimrod*, *Poetry Northwest*, *The Beloit Fiction Journal*, *Adirondack Review*, and *Briar Cliff Review*, among others. Her chapbook *Tree Forms* was published in 2011 by Finishing Line Press. Her essay "The Weight of a Human Heart" won *Memoir Journal*'s prize for the guns issue, Fall 2013. Her short story cycle *Letters from the Karst* is in search of a publisher. Olmsted is professor and head of the Diversity and Community Studies department at Western Kentucky, where she teaches graduate courses in Black Feminism and the Politics of Community, Utopias, Dystopias and Intentional Communities, and Place and the Problem of Healing. She lives in Bowling Green, Kentucky.

About the Cover Artist

I have known Yvonne Petkus for many years, as a colleague at Western Kentucky University, and as a wonderfully smart and nuanced thinker, whose large-bodied, partly-disintegrating women have always fascinated me. We met at a local coffee shop to talk about *Seeking the Other Side* and to look at images of her paintings, to see if they might resonate with the poems. I felt our friendship deepen in the intimacy of sharing what each of us hopes our art is doing.

In trying to summarize the poems for her, I spoke about tone, about loneliness and sorrow, but also affirming what I hope is true, that they are not naval-gazing poems, without joy or humor. I hope the poems come from a place of tenderness and compassion. Some of her paintings, *Braced* for sure, explore similar terrain. In an exhibition catalog, *Searching*, Kristina Arnold describes Petkus's work, noting how it "unashamedly confronts the physical and psychological effects of violence and the collective residue accrued both individually and as a society through repeated trauma." Yvonne described to me the repeated imagery of the woman coming into and going out of a visible sphere as evoking a process, about the becoming of self as many acts of courage or questing—expressions of a love of self that lets us love others, not the obsessive self that separates us from joy. While every book is a sort of journey, I cannot link poem to poem without emphasizing the importance of always becoming—"seeking" is a process, becoming its expression.

It is such a privilege and honor to have Yvonne's *Braced* as the cover image. My asking for the painting and her sharing of it are acts of reaching out, of connection, between image and word, painter and poet, book and painting, the framed and unframed. I hope my poems live up to what Yvonne says in her artist statement: "The underlying mechanism is an acknowledgement, a meditation, on the beauty and horror of the limitations of language. The overarching goal is to use visceral cues and a shifting surface as evidence of the larger human struggle—not in an ideal world but in this world."

In an interview, Yvonne responded to the question, "What recently made you smile?" with an answer I'd like to close with: "I recently hiked in Colorado with a good friend I hadn't seen in a long time and smiled the whole way." It reminds me of the trees I met in Colorado, the bristlecone pine and the others. Isn't compassion what allows us to meet the world with a smile?

Find more of Yvonne Petkus' work at http://www.yvonnepetkus.com/.

—Jane Olmsted

Fleur-de-Lis Press is named to celebrate the life
of Flora Lee Sims Jeter
(1901–1990)

⚜

www.ingramcontent.com/pod-product-compliance
Lightning Source LLC
Chambersburg PA
CBHW020902020526
44112CB00052B/1189